Animals of the World

Gray Wolf

By Edana Eckart

Children's Press®
A Division of Scholastic Inc.
New York / Toronto / London / Auckland / Sydney
Mexico City / New Delhi / Hong Kong
Danbury, Connecticut

Photo Credits: Cover © John Conrad/Corbis; p. 5 © D. Robert & Lorri Franz/Corbis; p. 7 © Renee Lynn/Corbis; pp. 9, 13 © Tom Brakefield/Corbis; p. 11 © W. Perry Conway/Corbis; p. 15 © Dale C. Spartas/Corbis; p. 17 © Lynda Richardson/Corbis; p. 19 © Chase Swift/Corbis; p. 21 © Layne Kennedy/Corbis
Contributing Editor: Jennifer Silate
Book Design: Mindy Liu

Library of Congress Cataloging-in-Publication Data

Eckart, Edana.
Gray wolf / by Edana Eckart.
p. cm. – (Animals of the world)
Contents: Gray wolf – Pups – Howls – New words – To find out more.
ISBN 0-516-24303-9 (lib. bdg.) – ISBN 0-516-27891-6 (pbk.)
1. Mexican wolf–Juvenile literature. [1. Mexican wolf. 2. Wolves.]
I. Title. II. Series.

QL737.C22E24 2003
599.773–dc21

2002153943

Printed in the United States of America.
1 2 3 4 5 6 7 8 9 10 R 12 11 10 09 08 07 06 05 04 03

Contents

1 Gray Wolf 4
2 Pups 10
3 Howls 16
4 New Words 22
5 To Find Out More 23
6 Index 24
7 About the Author 24

The **gray wolf** lives
in **forests**.

Gray wolves can be many colors.

Some are light brown.

Others are dark gray.

Gray wolves **travel** together.

A group of wolves is called a **pack**.

Young wolves are called **pups**.

The pups' parents take care of them.

Older wolves in the pack also take care of the pups.

Gray wolves eat **elk** and other animals.

A gray wolf **howls** to talk to other wolves.

Howls can be heard from far away.

Gray wolves are good runners.

They can run for a long time.

Gray wolves are very beautiful animals.

New Words

elk (**elk**) a type of large deer
forests (**for**-ists) large areas where many trees and other plants grow close together
gray wolf (**gray wulf**) a wild animal that looks like a large dog
howls (**houls**) when a dog or wolf makes a loud cry
pack (**pak**) a group of wolves
pups (**puhps**) wolves that are still young
travel (**trav**-uhl) to go from one place to another place

To Find Out More

Books
Wild, Wild Wolves
by Joyce Milton
Random House

Wolves
by Sandra Markle
Simon & Schuster Children's

Web Sites
Kids' Planet – Defenders of Wildlife: Gray Wolf
http://www.kidsplanet.org/factsheets/wolf.html
Learn about the gray wolf and enter a poster contest on this Web site.

Index

elk, 14

forests, 4

gray wolf, 4, 6, 8, 14, 16, 18, 20

howls, 16

pack, 8, 12

pups, 10, 12

run, 18

travel, 8

About the Author

Edana Eckart has written several children's books. She enjoys bike riding with her family.

Reading Consultants

Kris Flynn, Coordinator, Small School District Literacy, The San Diego County Office of Education

Shelly Forys, Certified Reading Recovery Specialist, W.J. Zahnow Elementary School, Waterloo, IL

Sue McAdams, Former President of the North Texas Reading Council of the IRA, and Early Literacy Consultant, Dallas, TX